salmonpoetry

*Publishing Irish & International
Poetry Since 1981*

ALSO BY MARY O'DONNELL

POETRY

Reading the Sunflowers in September (Salmon, 1990)
Spiderwoman's Third Avenue Rhapsody (Salmon, 1993)
Unlegendary Heroes (Salmon, 1998)
September Elegies (Lapwing, 2003)
The Place of Miracles, New & Selected Poems (New Island, 2005)
The Ark Builders (Arc Publications UK, 2009)
To the Winds Our Sails: Irish Writers Translate Galician Poetry,
co-edited with Manuela Palacios (Salmon, 2010)
Csodák Földje/Selected Poems Hungarian trans Kabdebó Tamás
(Irodälmi Jelen Könyvek, 2011, assisted by Literature Ireland)
Those April Fevers (2015, Arc Publications UK)

FICTION

Strong Pagans & other stories (Poolbeg, 1991)
The Light Makers (Poolbeg, 1992, 1993; 451 Editions 2018)
Virgin and the Boy (Poolbeg, 1996)
The Elysium Testament (Trident, 1999)
Where They Lie (New Island, 2014)
Storm over Belfast & other stories (New Island, 2015)
Sister Caravaggio (collaborative novel, Liberty Press, 2016)
Empire & other stories (Arlen House, 2018)

COMMENTARY

*Giving Shape to the Moment: the Art of Mary O'Donnell, Novelist, Poet &
Short-story writer*: Peter Lang, 2018. Contributors include Dr. Eibhear Walshe,
Dr. Anne Fogarty, Prof Pilar Vilar Argaiz, Prof Manuela Palacios, Éilís Ní Dhuibhne,
Ed. Dr. Elena Jaime de Pablos, Univ de Almeria, Spain.

More Praise for *Massacre of the Birds*

"What I admire most about Mary O'Donnell's poetry is the way she reaches beyond her formidable Irish roots to embrace, aesthetically and thematically, a global poetic that joins hands with Adrienne Rich, Federico García Lorca and Tomas Tranströmer. She blends the sensual with the mystical, the exotic with images from home. From finding the transcendent in something as simple as trying on a pair of sandals, to allowing imagination's flight in 'dancing to Cuban rhythms/ rum on my tongue,/a reek of skin, all body,/ burning up'— Mary O'Donnell takes us along with her on the journey of a life rooted in tradition, but too large to be contained."

RICHARD KRAWIEC

"In her new book Mary O'Donnell demonstrates a thrilling preparedness to breach boundaries and interrogate the world from fresh angles. The voice is urgent, with poems that can be both passionately political and devastatingly personal in turn, whether it is exploring the experience of refugees with 'a whole sea like a judgment on us', a woman's aging process or the writer's complex relationship with the art of poetry. There's anger with our casual plunder of the natural world and at our obliviousness to the suffering of those we seek to hide away. But there's also joy, a capturing the numinous—what O'Donnell calls the 'perfect stealth / of these moments'—when it offers itself in language that is precise, charged and hauntingly beautiful."

NESSA O'MAHONY

"Mary O'Donnell writes with the vigour and tremulous excitement of youth, now enriched with the wisdom of the years. Her lyricism is laced with raw courage and rare sinew, her compass being both meticulously local yet still global in its vision. In this astonishing collection, amongst many other subjects, her pen ponders upon the unwitnessed death of an aged aunt, the fancy skirts of an unwashed lettuce, the slaughter at Bataclan, with equal ease and elegance. As a poet, Mary O'Donnell stands with Heaney and Boland, Kavanagh and Clarke: as a living writer, she stands alone."

KEVIN MYERS

Massacre *of the* Birds

Mary O'Donnell

the arts council an chomhairle ealaíon

funding literature artscouncil.ie

Published in 2020 by
Salmon Poetry
Cliffs of Moher, County Clare, Ireland
Website: www.salmonpoetry.com
Email: info@salmonpoetry.com

ISBN 978-1-912561-28-5

Cover Artwork: *okeyphotos*
Cover Design & Typesetting: *Siobhán Hutson*

Printed in Ireland by Sprint Print

*Salmon Poetry gratefully acknowledges the support of
The Arts Council / An Chomhairle Ealaíon*

for Martin and Anna

Contents

Hanging House in a Canal

for Jean O'Brien

It lay on the other side,
the colour of country butter.
I longed to enter any way I could—
by door, window, chimney—
found it locked.
But there was a reflection,
clear as a mirror in the still waters,
the raised brows of dormer windows as it hung there,
upside down, the poking nose of the porch,
the comforting torso of walls.
I stripped off, knew immediately what to do,
dived, entered that beckoning house,
its bubbling whispers an embrace
as I burst through its porch reflection.
Now, within, I am drowning
in secrets, in the company of
rats, diving herons, grey roach
and crayfish.
With my own, as always.

Against the Vanishing

Hollywood Lake, Co Monaghan

1.

On the lakeshore
of conscience I stand.
God help me.

Certain that in Argentina,
a woman also stands,
nature-struck.

My unknown companion
will recognise waterfowl,
marvel at grebes, flamingos,

as I too greet the ducks
and moorhens
of this drumlin lake.

The wild pigs of her climate
still suck water
from thicketed reed-beds.

She sprays herself
against mosquitos, feels again
the deceptive rush of abundance.

2.

Here, Polish families picnic late
with children and a shaggy puppy.
Their voices echo, group to group.

Along the shore, two local men chat
about the swallows.
"Not so many th'year,"

one remarks, then bites into a sandwich.
Their murmurs reach me, sentiment
about shy birds from other decades—

corncrakes, cuckoos, long vanished,
and how, at this lake,
the pikes have overbred,

savaged every last cygnet.
"Shame", his companion adds,
finishing a beer.

A dusk fox slouches
from the wood, summer cubs in tow
as she prepares them for winter.

    3.

In Argentina, Saturday night falls
hours after I'm in bed. Even so,
a mirror conversation rumbles on,

thoughts replicate like pock-marks,
Where are the birds?
my unknown woman friend enquires,

What happened to the chinchilla,
the armadillo, giant otter?
And who last heard of any jaguars?

She bites into an olive,
sips her wine, reminds herself
to go again tomorrow to the lake.

4.

Years stretch and reverse.
Hard not to judge.
Argentina as much as Ireland,

Canada as much as France or Italy,
wherever birds are shot and feathers scatter.
See the white playboys

pose with rifles over zebra, elephant,
or cape buffalo,
as if this action was radiant.

Lucent cloud threaded behind trees
still cajoles. Briefly we believe
in the black reflection of a crannog,

its single surviving swan
creating a moment of ease.
But the seasons will not release us

from mounting debt.
On the lakeshore of living conscience
I stand.

I can do no other.

Buenos Aires Autumn

The trees here are playing with fire,
but on my island, the cold sap rises.
All day in this heat my flesh

is a violin, the strings melt
and are songless.
Something leaves me

or arrives, I cannot be certain.
The Rio de la Plata
sends mud-songs to the estuary,

intent on harmony with other rivers.
Eva Peron rests in La Recoleta,
where afternoon crowds leave posies

wrapped in paper, green string.
In Puerto Madero, the air is smokey
from the steakhouses

near the Puente de la Mujer,
the water of the Salado brown
with a sediment of base notes.

In Ireland, the rivers chant one note,
each minds its own sound-passage
to the sea, rises in wet spring-times

of fluted birch, nippled oak-buds
which will not soften until May.
In the south I feel the breath of a god

about to close passageways of air.
Sing on, some people say,
Be silent, say I, looking

to cross the equator in a rush of clouds
to the drenched hill-woods
and mire of my own fields.

A Husband's Lament for
the Massacre of the Birds

Of the five billion birds that fly through Europe each autumn
to spend winter in Africa and the warmer countries north of
the Mediterranean, up to one billion are killed by humans.

Newsweek, 02/07/2015

He does this by counting, he does this by digging.
O *loss, loss,* for the swallows have not returned,
loss, for the neap tide shows no sandpiper,
nor greenshank, and he digs the garden to plant
what will attract all comers of wing.
All are welcome in his green field, the swifts
that have not returned to criss-cross the sky,

pigeons long shot and bagged,
and songbirds that in Europe are vanishing—
glued, poisoned, trapped—so that the full-bellied
can dine in a rustic restaurant in Tuscany.
He welcomes too in his garden dream
the fan-tailed warbler, glued to death in Cyprus
in an agony of open beak—chaffinch, blackcap,

quail and thrush—O *loss, loss,* as the songs die,
and little throats close against the final mutilation.
He will continue to prepare each year this place
for the birds, and surely a man can beat his chest
and cry out to his neighbour, *Let us bellow in rage,*
let us bellow in sorrow, let us plant these spaces
to make havens for the hunted.

Gaia, April 2020

for Liz Sherry

The first time I heard the word
was in 1983. A young mother

new to the workshop,
baby in arms: This is *Gaia,*

she said.
Now Gaia, bearer of life,

rests in our arms again.
Her supple fists release

thrush and finch
as novelties, she tosses

bees towards uncut,
swollen dandelions,

fondles wood-anemone
in neglected copses.

Her hand cracks yellowness
like an egg, a broken spill

on each dawn. She has
cleansed the thick silts

of canals, muds
of the Rio de la Plata,

the scum of the Liffey,
so that fish may return.

All day, cherry-trees twitch
along tawny terraces,

as sparrows dart
on sprays of pink.

At dusk, her eyes show us
how to gaze higher, deeper:

this haul of stars, brighter—
more of them—guiding the eye

through Hawking's cosmos,
with no reverence for anything

except themselves in expansion.
Gaia sucks at the breast,

drowsing while we
stay home and fret,

the anxiety of parenthood
filling us with duties,
obligations.

The Little Waves, like Judgements

Near the third beach beyond the town,
The Syrians have arrived with baggage
And chattels of their journeys.
The people say *Welcome to Sweden,*
You are safe here. This winter in Visby,
They live in holiday chalets; already,
They walk the seafront with shopping bags,
With clear faces. They will not be hungry
Or thirsty, hounded like sewer rats.
With what dignity they walk.
As if nothing had happened,
And they come unmarked,
Their faces knowing only the future.
Their boys are playing football
In the grass beneath gunmetal, bare trees.
Next summer, their children will swim
On the warm shoreline, tossed
By the little waves, shingle and sand,
A whole sea like a judgement on us,
Sea boulders like full stops at sunset.

Message from Malmö

In the market the immigrants
are grappling with clothes,
some to buy, some to sell.
Everybody has something on offer,
a garment or some coins.
The faces of the Syrians, new to the place,
show intent. They are here. They have made it.
Now some sort of life may begin again.
The women wear sadness in their eyes,
thick as the heavy wool garments for sale;
the husbands are cloaked in defiance,
desperation; and the young men, also
defiant, wear invisible undergarments
that sparkle with hope; they are girded
by belts of adventure, possibility,
preparing to mend the great torn blanket
that was once their family, now
left behind in the dust.

Direct Provision and the Old Agricultural College Ghosts

We meet on the stretch between two crossroads:
dark-haired schoolchildren,
sturdied in jackets and hats for the town
three miles away, their families bunked up
in the old agricultural college.

In this place, spirits loiter—of young men
who once handled sheep and cattle in pens,
raising them for market
to a clang of feeding buckets, disinfectant smells,
the scrape of shovels
in the dung-lumped byres.

I've heard music from the yard in summer,
the thud of a football as boys play
for homelands: Albania, Moldova,
Nigeria, attempting perhaps to forget
half-dreamt voices on night corridors,
to silence a ghostly bleating and lowing at dawn,
as they themselves become invisible.

The Blackbird, God Almighty, and Allah

(Remembering the dead children of Syria, murdered by Bashar al Assad)

There you are again this bitter spring,
taking position at crown of birch.
You hold forth like God Almighty,
or Allah, fresh arrived to change terrible places
to green-shook and calm.

      Listening to you,
all bright breast, slick-song, you'd swear
that religions were ready at last
for a pagan such as you or me,
to offer natural gospel,
a peaceful Qu'ran

.

.

.

      but world is never ready
for melodies of yellow beak, the glossed
feather of your black sleekness
testing its mettle, proving year on year,
that when the bones
have crumbled
within shallow graves,
      you still return
and offer a dance of dances, sparking euphony—
automatic as dawn, inevitable as sunset.

      Do not bless me, God or Allah—
no need while in the garden
      lives this Most High creature.

Muse

after Ted Hughes's 'The Thought Fox'

He lives in the wild brackens
beyond the garden.

I must stay alert,
alone, resist the cosmetic clatter
of an evening of too many useless acts.

Pointless to tempt him with inscribed saucers
of scallops, marbled blue cheese,
or the Omega of bone marrow.

His appetite is not sated on such
fine produce. As he springs silently,
rank as a goat, through the rime frost
and a chink in the porch window,
I inhale the funk of him,
sense his stealth, have known it
all my life.

He stands at my back, caresses my arm,
the one that cramps with the pain of staying put,
his one silver hoof tapping a line, a rhyme,
on the floorboards.

He scarcely whispers, yet, bothered
by his absence these sullen months,
I hear him clearly.

Hush now (such sibilant breaths)
I have broken the fences, the safe arbours
that restrained you, have torn down
the walls
that bound you to silence.

I twitch to answer, accepting
his hand-curl around mine. In an instant,
our fingers shift across the moonlit desk.

Heron and the Women

Quiet and still,
those mornings when walkers
suddenly pounce, with dogs
ripping muscular through the wind
on the far side of the canal.

Female voices,
he hears their heat as
if released.
He is a study in grey
a match for the silence
absent in their words.

When they see him,
it's too late. He has lifted,
spread his wings
against gravity, above
the careless spirals of words.

Sometimes,
they witness the grace
of wing-tilt and wind,
the dangling twig legs.

Ancient symbols appear,
as on a page,
to remain unread,
wet inks of a script dropped
from above as he flies,
to settle only, when dogs
are restrained,
and the canal is vellum.

Ghost

I want to be a ghost in my own house.
You may still live here, you can come and go
in the casual glide of daily tasks.
Just leave me be, happy in my haunting
of this room, which has never had a key.

The secret metal is my writer's heart,
which needs to shrink away from signs of flesh,
becoming white, then paler, less than grey,
so that you hardly notice how greatly
I need this house to submit to haunting,

to inhale my chill. If I am unseen
yet felt, surely that will be sufficient.
I want to be a ghost in my own house.
Do not speak to me. Do not spread fond hands
Along my thigh or breast, just come and go.

Be free. I am haunting myself away
from open doors and friendly passageways,
from that candled nook by a winter fire,
withdrawing behind the shades of morning,
while you inhabit the shell I bequeath.

Twenty Inches of Hair

He arrives weekly,
after dawn when the green pigeons feed
on figs, seeds, yesterday's specks of rice.

This is what a wife does;
for the children, for her keep, besides,
wives are expensive. With such hair,
other men will desire her.

The agent cuts, first to her ears,
having measured
from nape of neck to base of spine,
where the sacred serpent rests.
But her Kundalini,
curled within its chill of poverty,
does not rise to meet her spirit.
Beads of sweat gather at her neck
as he cuts, then cuts some more,
the dark fronds tumble to a metal bowl.
Finally, his blade: from the crown down,
skin-shearing until skull is revealed,
bald as a peacock's egg.

Some woman will thank you,
the agent mumbles
(He gathers the hair, wipes the bowl).
They will bleach the sacks
of blue-black hair from India
for the pleasure of a woman with blue eyes.
Extensions, the agent assures her,
the latest thing in England.

Money changes hands, agent to husband.
Rapidly, she draws the dupatta
over her shamed head.
The agent leaves. Outside,
a peacock cries *eeeiu, eeeiu.*
Her husband returns, swings two green pigeons
from his fingers. *Today's meat,* he murmurs,
avoiding her eye, places them,
curl-clawed, beaks oozing,
in the bowl that held her hair.

The Hairdresser's Lament

I never thought I'd have a private gig
like this: a plea for a house visit,
information leaked in whispers.
An infant. A Spanish swimming-pool.
Would I dress the mother's hair,
prior to the funeral?

I see her already, bent and white
over a kitchen sink, my fingertips pressing lightly
to her scalp, as with all my women's heads.
I'm told I give a good massage.
But never before like this. Her abundant hair:
already shorn of sanity.

On the phone, she whispered something
about hair loss—already—fistfuls losing grip.
But I'll shield her, I'll raise her roots
with back-combing, a gloss of coppery furls
cheek-brushing like the wings
of a safe casement against her dark.

The car chugs through November fog,
I'm chewing cigarettes as I squint
to check the details: the kid-skin bag—
my brushes, combs, colorants, conditioners—
whatever it takes to create a weave
of mourning hair, for her to look like a mother,
as her child might view her if he could.

As I tilt the steering-wheel to her high gates
and home, the years of women's heads
flash before me: upside-down as I rinse clear—
their smiling waxed eyebrows, wet temples,
closed eyes with centipede lashes
as necks relax, and hairs slip down to matt
in the plughole like drowning voles.

It Wasn't a Woman

who used a stick to abort the baby in an 11-year-old girl
who gang-raped a 14-year-old
who opened a woman to a room of shamrock green rugby shirts,
later texting about *spit roast* and *sluts*
who gave money to a rag-picker
took one of her five children to a faraway brown-dust city
who sold her on to the businessmen
it wasn't a woman who beat the child with an iron bar
so that vertebrae were crushed
it wasn't a woman who ruptured the rectum of a small boy
who broke the vagina of a baby girl
it wasn't a woman
who scalded a wife because she spoke to another man
who flung acid in the face of a girl who did not want to marry
who poured caustic soda on a wife's genitals
in a quiet Irish town
it wasn't a woman
who broke a nose blackened an eye
bit a cheek so that the marks of those teeth
are tell-tale pits in the skin and her breasts are purple and green
it wasn't a woman who punched the baby out of her
so she bled to death
it wasn't a woman who rejected those twin girls
it wasn't a woman who burned a widow to death
who shouted at a wife in the rich people's shopping mall
who later forced her to have sex took the children away
kept all the money
who called out names like *dog* and *here, bitch,*
who put a collar around her neck
then led her on all fours around a golden apartment
it wasn't a woman who smashed photo frames
and perfume bottles who kept a gun beside the bed
and threatened to use it
who blamed her even as he punched her

roared the rhythms of *cunt-face cunt-face cunt-face*
because it helped hit her harder
it wasn't a woman
it wasn't a woman
it wasn't a woman

#MeToo, 12 Remembered Scenes and a Line

1968, County Wexford, the light flick
of the Colonel's hand up my summer dress
as I dart from the hotel stairwell;

1970, Leeson St, the priest
with a November evening burning appetite
for PG Wodehouse, by my hospital bed;

1971, a lift home from a stranger,
Emyvale Road. I fight to leave, he reaches over
to squeeze my breast, I strike out and he swears;

1972, carnival, Fermanagh, a disembodied hand
shoots through the crowd, grabs my left breast;

1973, Leeson Park in spring, snowdrops, moss
at the base of trees, an open raincoat,
shock of white, the dark-stemmed pubis;

1974, Maynooth, a parked yellow Renault,
snail-trail of spunk on his thigh as I pass;

1976, Monaghan, a struggle in a car,
his sweet aftershave, his sweat.
He is small; I am strong enough.

1980, Croke Park, All Ireland Offaly-Kerry
Semi-final, crotch-groped on crammed
concrete steps outside the toilets;

1980, Heidelberg in soft rain, sage-green hills,
the Prof stares at my polo-neck t-shirt,
breathes too close, murmuring 'provokativ';

1986, the throng of Antalya bus station, Turkey,
sips of hot sweet tea, then crotch-groped;

1994, *le Metro*, between Solferino and Rue du Bac,
crotch-groped in a crammed carriage;

2010, Sant'agnello, between two cars
a young man stands unzipped,
hand frantic as my daughter and I pass by.

I was never raped.

Finding 'Our Place' Heroic

for Maria Macklin

In an article in the Irish Independent on May 6, 1937, Fine Gael TD John A. Costello claimed that the draft Constitution "allows a wide latitude" for the introduction of gender discrimination. The following day, the newspaper's women's correspondent, Gertrude Gaffney, went further, claiming that de Valera "dislikes and distrusts us as a sex, and his aim ever since he came to office has been to put us in what he considers is our place."

*

Katie O'Toole, Carbury,
rises at six, dresses infants for crèche,
    fills washing-machine, slow cooker
        set for 7pm Monday evening.

Annemarie Tuomey, Moone,
lives in a hotel room, studies for her Leaving.

Jessica Macken, Kildangan,
Her words flow early morning, her tapping keyboard;
    Outside, the wind cracks the birch branches.

Becky O'Brien, traveller,
imprisoned in China for teaching in two schools
        instead of one, strip-searched,
            phone confiscated.

Elizabeth Raymond, traveller,
reaches Everest base camp on September 13,
        pictures on Facebook.

Trish Murray, seamstress,
hillocks of strewn fabric in her garage studio,
        unsettled by the night fox outside her window.

Danute Balkus, Palmerstown,
cycles to the Financial Quarter, rain on her face,
senses money-moods in the eyes
of the MBAs.

Molly Gilboy, Kildangan,
raves quietly after a morning of minding her mother.
Will marry Jessica Macken next April.

Mags Murnaghan, Nurney,
pharmacist, body like a litmus strip to the smell
of a clean man's sweat.

Anne McGrath, Lackagh,
whose husband plays her like a drum with his fist
on Saturday nights.

Caoimhe Mulkerns, Killanny, three jobs,
Airbnb, four children in school, fashion
consultant, local baker, planning Christmas
in Byron Bay.

Bella McEnroy, Portobello, packs a bag
for Holles Street, unintended pregnancy,
wants to walk beneath the trees
on Merrion Square.

Tracy Byrne, Rathconnell,
sex-worker, red dress, animal print thong,
occasional escort in a Dublin 5-star.

June Devlin, Ballyvarney,
begs on Grattan Bridge, has twins in the Rotunda,
cries "Mammy, O Mammy!"

Adaku Adebayo, Maynooth,
introduced to father's friends at ten,
observed by her teachers.

Bridget Deeney, Walterstown,
plants a holly hedge, lunches with friends,
books an appointment for Botox
the Monday after her father dies.

Sorcha Feighery, Fairview,
three jobs to pay for college, fries burgers,
trains for the Liffey Swim.

Reading Hour in the St. Louis Girls' Library

for Mary Hosty

I knew Narcissus lived on at the crannóg lake
within the grounds. Smitten by his own exquisite head,

line of jaw, a sublime bottom lip made to suck,
bite, or kiss, he ignored the cries of curlews

from November's glinting reed-beds.
Here too was Leda, undone by that brazen swan,

who drifted around the crannóg in disguise,
all dipped head, quickened eye.

Subtle the shift, fingers at first bewitched by depth
of feather, until her thighs unlocked to the rip

of his cock, then clouds of confusion
as she crawled away.

Worst was meddling Cupid, shooting
gold tips to stir Apollo's lust for Daphne,

whom he struck with lead. Pursuer and pursued,
Apollo's groin-soak never found release: she, feeling

no desire—an eternal virgin—stayed resolute as oak.

Communion Day, 2001

Constellations of frost netting the pavement.
I bolt towards the internet café,
so intent on a writer's junket in Katumba
that I've crossed a hemisphere and missed
her First Communion.
                    So much for silence
and words, the white robe of art. And now,
as photos download in slow slivers on the screen,
the bitter spike of loss: for here is her body shape,
ghostly until images are complete.

I sip my coffee, unnerved
by the full unfolding spectacle, ivory white,
a trembling veil and crown of florets;
they've prepared her well for this rite,
snowdrop fresh, silken purse on wrist.

Her father stands close, smiling,
grandparents widen the wings of her protection.
She's happy. But I'm not present,
having forfeited the radiant hour.
I trudge back to the writers' house,
resenting friends who urged me to leave,
hear my mother's truth all the way from Ireland:
You'll regret it for the rest of your days.
Above me, cockatoos flocking home to roost
fill the dusk whitely.

On reading my Mother's Sorrow Diary

(The counsellor said "God wanted him".
"I wanted him more", she replied and left).

The diary was the thing, labelled
Sorrow, no laughter in these pages,
double underlined.

I expected smoking syntax, tirades
against her daughters. Instead, she wrote of loss,
the felling of trees; herself split in two

and feeling useless, but happy when we visited,
happier still if we were happy.
She despised the holiday with us, her idea;

Never again, to a car journey from Malaga
to Jeréz (filthiest town I've ever seen),
and she'd scream if my husband attempted

Spanish one more time, his *Gracias Senõrs*
alarm-bells of grating over-eagerness
within the fortress of her well-travelled

knowledge. Mostly, she wrote from day to day.
A good day. Did some shopping.
God when will this end, when will we be together?

She blessed us, her daughters;
her paper refused harsh words, what there was,
scrupulously overlaid with her code,

an apple, an apple, an apple,
the surefire way to make illegible.
We remained her lovely girls, no slight to us

while even in grief she edited herself.

New Year's Eve, 1958

Midnight. The Adeste wavered across the air
from the Protestant Church in the town square.
The streets were silent in a watermark of frost.

She sat with her father, hours dead,
in the yellow room; below, her brothers murmured
in the range-hot kitchen, the kettle singing
as tea was poured. Earlier, her fingers
squeezed the dry sponge that moistened his lips
in the thickened final moments.
Body now waxy, face smooth,
he fell away to join other family ghosts,
where conversation would be rich,
contrary to all they'd known in life.

She still kept the red shoes he'd gifted her.
Alone, she guarded the span of her life within his,
as the New Year pealed in, rolling her
towards January's grey minutes.

Mother, I am Crying

I feel the fire in your mind,
undimmed though the body betrays.
Northwards again, the car hammers up the M1,

near neolithic passage graves, and yet undug
ancestral plains. In the distance, Carlingford Lough,
mountains hollowing to meet the coast.

Thoughts drift to the story of Maeve and the Táin Bó
Cualainge, and I marvel at the power of women,
used and ill-used. Then, the first anxious strand

of wondering how you are, will be, and outcomes
unimaginable. When I arrive all is as usual:
the gradual dereliction of what was once a pristine place.

The weekend is spent in doing—too much—I know
that all you want is time, not acts—less cleaning-up,
less scouring of the fridge or emptying cupboards.

The lids of jam jars have long expired their date.
Within, blue mould glows resentfully at me,
intruding daughter. I chat with you,

although some part is silent as I observe
your body, so tilted now, and crumpled fingers,
clumsy with knives and forks; the barked feet

and coiled-tight toes, nails thick as claws.
You refuse my kneeling to tend them,
rebuff aromatic oils, or cooling peppermint.

Before I leave we visit the grave, where you pray
a moment, fingers clenched to my arm.
I regard the hill that shoulders above us,

remembering a pair of swans that crossed,
the day that he was buried. All your passion amounts
to this: the life you had together, in which children

never quite equalled the sum of two parts, a rule
of nature. Later, the car whizzes past the Hill of Tara,
crowned in full May bloom. I think of the long dead,

and all that sunken ground,
what shifts beneath us
                         even as we live.

On Metaphor

I never realised how apt
those old comparisons of female parts

to roses in particular—metaphysical lines
on love, lushness and moisture,

or petals in tactile frills—until the day
I soaped and washed my mother

in her shower-chair,
saw her labia in their dying glory.

Like any late autumn rose,
her petals, hanging loose, had shrivelled,

awaiting the slightest wintry wind
to blow them free.

Even so, I write of them with love,
the metaphysics of a woman's

life in transit, this aged Venus
eclipsed by time.

My Mother Remembers her Irish

Like Alice, she has fallen down the rabbit hole.
In a room at the bottom,

rejecting a bottle labelled DRINK ME,
she reaches for the cracked urn of language:

SPEAK ME, it invites.
White hair in disarray, she unstops it.

The contents fizz up and over the lip of glaze
as she recovers the sounds she forgot

after schooling. Now, she has broken away
from the language bunker,

its torqued English,
takes to speech at the midnight hour.

As if fighting the Jabberwocky,
she uses old songs to push against a paralysis

of chair-lifts, walking frames,
they emerge on her tongue, ancient oratorio:

síolta; beidh aonach amárach; cad dúirt tú,
a chailín álainn? Ba mhaith liom dul abhaile.

Such softness that rarely found its way in English,
now honeys her tongue in the magical flight of dotage.

Time, released, enriches conversation.
"Did you know that this Republic was born

70 years ago today? Years after the Maglioccos
in the town taught me Mussolini's anthem"

We speak of Easter music, the St. Matthew Passion,
her *ceol cráifeach*. She wonders

if the sun will dance, Easter Sunday morning,
on the hill above her house at Kilnadrain,

where she wants to return sometime soon.
  Mo thinteán féin, she adds.

My Mother says No on Bloomsday

It is not easy, it is not easy
to wheel an old woman to the shower

on Bloomsday, when the world
and Molly cry *yes, yes, yes,*

and she is saying *no, no, no,*
because what's left of her life

depends on the freedom of No.
How Joycean of her

to resist the cleaned-up conscience
of filial attention, your need

to fix her taints and odours,
wash hair and teeth,

attend to toes when all she wants
is to float on the lily-leaf of her own

green bedspread, drowsing Molly
in a tangle of snow-white hair.

Now, dreams enclose her
more than talk of showers or meals,

the flowing waters of memory
rise and touch her skin

just where the mattress eases
spine and bones

in that yellow-walled room.
Hello, my darling, she greets

his photograph, flinging kisses
towards mottled frame.

To her then,
the logic of love,

to her, the logic of *No,*
her tongue untameable.

Aunt Mary in the Nursing Home

Like an accountant,
her quill-sharp mind still oversees the bills
as I sign off for her again.
Thin skin loosens in folds on her skeleton;
her hands have bruises.
She's deaf,
      can't eat,
              eyesight's poor.
The day-room scene upsets her:
slack mouths,
      the permanently raving,
            all marble-eyed stares.

In sunny weather, hatted residents cluster
outside near bright begonias.
Nurses encourage her to join
flower-arranging,
      No! she says
with a wave of that pianist's hand,
      No! she shakes her head
at the slow excruciation
      of an Irish céili waltz,
removes her hearing aids.
On the September night she dies,
      the nursing home
           scarcely shudders
               in its coma.

The Dumpster

Crucifixes drop with brute speed
down the metal shaft:

the black foreboding one from Santander
hits the bottom, heavy as a brick,

then the metallic clank
of a cross from Medjugorje,

Lourdes assortments, a ripple of rosaries.
Unfair to think her merely devout:

nieces and nephews lived their lives
un-preached at by her, who held her distance

from women's rites—marriage and birth.
The load bulked high, we secure with ropes,

await the trundling truck to ferry her chattels—
ornaments, chairs, an unused card-table,

sheet music and manuscripts,
Gregorian chant, folk songs, a broken violin.

I watch now from her gateway,
as the dumpster lumbers uphill

on this spring-green country road.
Judas-like, my silver-tinged command

is to take her precious things away.
She is eight months dead.
Hedges and birdsong extol the day.

Limpet

On her left side, she sometimes feels
her husband's slow heartbeat through the mattress,
steady at 60 a minute, an athlete's rhythm.

Hers is erratic, loses sequence and rhyme,
when all around, hormones dance
to circadian time: seasonal,
annual, and to everything its hour.

She is like a limpet, suctioned to rocks
as the sea hammers down.
Holding fast during the backwards sloosh,
she shivers as the outgoing roar
siphons her chambers.

The minutes are drowning, her heart knows it,
walls enlarged as a crimson tide
forces its tongue through her time-piece.

And like a limpet, she awaits the cruel blade
that, finally, will pierce beneath,
impaling the muscle so that it shrivels,
as she homes at last to tide and flowing foam.

Cherry Trees

The cherry trees are hauling their pink burden
through April. Plausible as Judas,
branches engorged with the quick exchange
of beauty for loss as we watch the blossoms,

so soft, so dense, so briefly in their prime.
All week I have hauled a weighted pain,
my body crammed tight, dressed with petals,
the sight of which sting my eyes pink-raw.

This week especially, the world teems
with cherry trees about to spill death
in crowning circles like tinted snow,
concealing Easter thorns.

The Blackwater at Ballyalbany Bridge

On the shallow riverbank, water sucks
at tufts of moss and willow, branches throw
calligraphies of shade at passing water-hens.

From the low-arched bridge, tawny waters
I once imagined inscribe a journey
to Lough Neagh of the eels; I threw paper boats,

rushed to watch them from the other side,
white nibs scribbling upstream.
An un-noted river, but purposeful,

a slim brown god, slow-soaking Drumlin silt,
it caresses trout, then flicks at dipping fern.
The kind of place where myths are formed

by people set to punt on other waters,
away from quick speech, the parochial puddle.
I too wanted something else, and remember:

this river, scarcely deep enough to drown in,
floated dreams I could not then decipher.
They flickered on the surface of the shallows.

It took me years to write them into practice.

Homewards across the Bog of Allen

The same weekly trip, bypassing towns, quick tics of winking windows
from a distant village where the sun glints. You're distracted by etiolated clouds
in late afternoon, when sun breaks between one road sculpture and the next:

bog oak and six moon phases, all copper burnish, starkly lit. Your life
amounts to segments of waxing and waning, where even decline is growth,
and finds dignity. Behind the moons, the lipped bog, hickory brown, then stacked banks

where the *sleán* cuts deep. You'd stop the car if you could, tumble into a heartland
where no village or town can grow, the rapacious wind composing long notes
in winter's fret, the birch, the rowan—here a lament, there a reel.

Further out, the composition of ancient self continues— a blackened slurch of turf,
wild to the end. No grief here as some bog-imp digs up, wriggles out, lifts and tucks you
to itself, fondles your spirit in the sun's final flicker, ferries you, almost virgin,

like a gift to the planes of night.

Photograph, Painting, Poem

I wanted to show the world my lettuces
and broad beans, their hopeful, sweet green,
fresh from the garden in July.

The lettuce lay unwashed,
leaves crimped like the hems of fancy skirts,
while some of the beans nestled unzipped

in a blue colander. But the ones I'd released
tumbled on a wooden board, like embryos
in jade. Straightaway, I uploaded

a picture onto Facebook, so friends could note
such trumpeting lettuce, such demure beans.
Half way across the world, Rita pressed Like,

then painted the lettuces and beans.
Now, my photograph and her art shimmer
together, shifts of white and sage-green

show how young the beans that day
before lunch, when we just sat and talked
and a block of pollen-gold light on the kitchen floor

deceived us, saying the world was right,
and good, unfolding as it should.
I bought Rita's painting. Today in the kitchen,

my lettuces and broad beans hang hopeful
as winter draws in.

A Report to the Home Galaxy on 'Speck'

1. At night, the sensitives are aware of light years travelled.
When Speck is visible, the principle of recovery
is purely gravitational. Wave-borne across space,
the stillborn, ectopic, or not needed,
emit from a billion galaxies.
In some sectors, they call it womb, or belly.
With us who observe the phenomenon,
'speck' is a preferred citation.

2. Speck's elements are tumbled centrifugally in deep space,
as miscarried and terminated parts.[1] Other composites
include toe joints or hooves, sealed eyelids, the whisk of first fur[2].
For some, it is another chance; for others, an unformed thing
is never thus, but fully imagined. In Speck, they are enfolded—
skulls, a coccyx, a calf's muzzle or half-opened, oneiric eye.

3. To be here—the agreed thing—to have been created
into existence and attach to earth-life, is its own vitality.
For the majority, there is no agitation, although the sensitives,
largely female, are aware of constant rhythm. It sweeps osmotically
through their skins; they stir to cellular recognition,
consider what place their Speck, once ferried in endometrium,
cushioned by pinopodes[3] (now lost), in their arms
on their earth.

NOTES:

[1] This mélange of limbs, craniums,
minuscule elbows would, in average circumstances, have clung
to the interior walls of females.

[2] Eyebrows, eyelashes not yet formed.

[3] Small, finger-like protrusions from the endometrium

Sharing a Car with Patrízia

Her personal driver is mostly silent,
hair glossed, shirt ironed.
Occasionally, they murmur a few words.

From the rear seat
I am conducting their private lives
as his hands nudge the steering-wheel
through traffic on the bridge,
above the Tietê. Thunder-clouds

snag the sky-scaling apartments
of the wealthy, and São Paulo
turns purple. We pass the walled-in homes
of eminences—the Mayor, some army man,
and that of a famous singer.

Autumn has arrived, solemn clouds
are permitted, touching as they do the souls
of watchers like me, or street people
stretched out in Cracolândia,
who will not feel the rain as it strikes.

Again, an exchange in Portuguese.
Her ruby necklace
flushes as evening darkens,
and thunder breaks.

The Men I Once Knew

for Anna

They offered gifts, like male penguins
in courtship. One offered a bag of lemons,
bright and warm from the Mediterranean garden
where he plucked them. Another took me
on a boat. It had no life-jackets.
We sailed dangerously, I was sea-sick for hours.
No problem, he said, *just watch the horizon.*
The third kept painting me, *Botticelli's Venus,*
he murmured, digging his brush
to the canvas, failing each time to find a line
to match the line of my thigh.

Lemons. Life-jacket. A canvas.
We failed calamitously,
but even now on any day,
I can't say I ever felt ruined
by their attentions.
It was how we passed the time,
pleasantly.

Sandals

The last time someone fitted a pair of sandals
was in Camden Street. I remember
how his fingers caressed beneath
the arches of my feet, how they slipped
around my ankles as he found the strap,
fastened it, then glanced up, teasing out
my approval of something other
than sandals. "They suit you!" he said, and soon
I danced from the shop, out into market stalls,
the red straps soft on my ankles,
feet cool against new leather
as the sun beat down through traffic fumes,
the afternoon alive as I moved past the crates
of oranges, persimmons, bright red peppers.

Trimming the Ivy

My beloved, when I asked him
to trim the ivy on the house,

in his zeal forgot to stop.
Now the house is naked,

her white chest exposed.
Perhaps it's better

to see her skin and bone,
the long tendrils of a plant

in death, brown-veined
while medicinal wind

makes ready
her wintry finery.

Meeting on Parnell Square

for Mary Guckian

It was good to see you
after all this time,

a cancer growing,
you said, and days

in hospital, outcome
uncertain, though all

not lost. You shove
your latest poetry in my hand,

fuse of a gypsy soul
that knows to take life lightly

around the drawl
of heavy buildings.

Between us, we still avoid
wrong entrances,

cross the road for coffee
on the next corner,

laughing at a lone figure,
stalking in his tatter.

St Stephen's Green

The young lie around
as we once did—

sprawled like beached starfish
as they take the sun—

though it's April and cool.
This—the lunchtime round,

beneath pink flowering cherries,
near ducks and pond,

far from women bound
for clothing missions—

must be freedom.
Sun-squinting, they surely

know at what distance
they hover. Beyond the trees

working buildings call out,
and a slow tram waits.

Telling a Friend about Reading Lorca in the Alhambra

for Mary O'Keeffe

This was happiness, I said.
We talked about the quick, perfect stealth
of those moments. I sat beneath orange trees,
and the ground breathed up on me.
A gentle possession, a lover
long known, rarely seen.

And later, when the sun had set that day,
a full moon stealing over the Sierras,
I thought of going to Santiago de Cuba,
as he had done,
of dancing to Cuban rhythms
rum on my tongue,
a reek of skin, all body,
burning up—

Those Prostitutes in Cuba

They were like two kittens, he said,
snuggling up to him,
they were fun and they liked him.

I thought—against my own sex—how
enviable his freedom to fall in
with such company, then breakfast

with them afterwards, heartily, admiring
their health, their strong teeth, that
vitality. It could never happen

to a woman my age, two tiger men
who would not wound, the three of us
so human in a dusky room, sunlight

stealing through the slats in colours
from Matisse, the riotous world
within and without.

Remembering Amsterdam

for Manuela Palacios

Those canal streets, like a carnival of hope,
with tourists wearing masks: Wife. Husband.
Something for all the family! a man calls out
like a brother, gesturing inside.

We trek on beneath festoons of coloured lights.
Reds and yellows quiver in a lisping breeze, festive
compared to the Dublin canals, where women slope,
lost curs in the dark.
Here, everything is wholesome.

On one street, you draw me forwards—
it's 1987, we have not seen the like.
Other men press close before each window,
as if watching television.

Such women. Dusky skin, white skin,
smiles (not just any come-hither), for each of us,
their eyes gleaming.

They recline in gift-boxes
within a theatre of light as our eyes
travel their flesh, explorers tracking
the blood-pinked belly of golden antelope,
hooves striking sparks.

My eyes too, mesmerised by magic,
coveting it. And I swear one of them meets my gaze,
reads my betrayal of her and our kind.

I know then I am no different,
no *wife, Weib, or vīf.* Since then,
I sometimes climb into a special gift-box,
in solidarity with the woman,
who still meets my gaze.

On Soft-grazing Sea Cows &
other Creatures of the Deep

An unmodelled civility of soft-grazing Sea Cows
does not harm the sub-oceanic dwellings of lesser creatures,
nor threaten nor savage. Gentle grazers of earth's bottoms,
coal black bull, his cow and calf: not derided for stupidity.
And mermaids who fail to adjust to the habits of land,
find cruelty there, keep the people at a remove
by warning of women with red hair,
menstruating women, and those with child,
to avoid the boats.
They long for our men to dote on them,
pitch a song-cry of orgasm from beneath the waves,
as they did at Odysseus, his celibate crew,
their cocks straining against the sirens.
And great-muscled sea-horses with fish tails,
and hooves like fins, when come to soil
cannot be outraced once their land-legs steady.
Yet on the strand, at high tide,
they ride again on shifting spume,
spindrift saliva from their tender muzzles
lacing the waves.

Know also of the barnacle goose
that *openeth the shell by degrees, till at length*
it is all come foorth, and hangeth onely by the bill;
in short space after it commeth to full maturitie,
and falleth into the sea, where it gathereth feathers
is birthed from a barnacle shell, not an egg:
a bird-fish capable of the darkest dives,
all quickened body from wave clutch and push.

Finally, also, phantom homesteads of the drowned,
at Bannow, Lahinch, Inishmore and Cemaes Head,
pounded below by tidal-shriek, storm-broken cliffs,
inhabited by drifts of mermaids seeking mates;
and sea-cows and the like, nosing through the sunken
dwellings. All windows and doors are agape—
nor church bells ring out, while creatures of the deep
graze here, drift, feel safe.

Nocturnal

In the winter garden
at full moon.
I watch the fields
turn to watered silk,
a chemise for the ghosts of me;
sense the pace of a journey,
steady and slow,
across constellations,
across my skin.

Barefoot,
my toes ease out,
loosen to pale fish-tails.
Nobody sees, and I float,
released.

We are not so alone, after all.
I can praise the moon, which bears
the tick of my tired mind,
the worn churn of sadness;
in this light I can praise a tree,
solitary at last,
so I stretch myself around the bole,
arms now glittering dorsals,
and still, nobody sees.

I am dropped on a song line
to this reef home.
It holds me on secret shelves of light,
bushes by day, now filmy cushions
that flimmer sea-green.
Moon and trees,
lit to new shapes,
the lobe of my darker self
swimming free.

I am all tail and fin,
scales bulge with weight of words,
my fugitive grace.
There is nothing but
this rhythm, rocking,
rocking . . .

Crow Knowledge

By All Hallows, the sympathy of crows
fills the evening air as light fades, and souls
warm thin feet against a screen of blazing birch.

They falter across a field of winter corn,
bewildered, on an earth no longer theirs.
How they long to lie abed, as tight in flesh

as crows are in feather, ruffed together,
still bound to life. But the scald crows warn:
this day and no further may you roam.

Clearing skies make way for gods of frost,
souls shiver at the memory of fires,
wines, red meat. They recall smiles too

and themselves, once, raucous as the crows
that scold them now. These black guardians
tilt low, call 'Time!' with beak and claw.

As November's shim-clouds lock
beneath the horizon, their dark wings ferry
the malingerers to eternity's twig-dark roost.

A Poem from Gotland

13th November 2015

It was a day of boredom and the words would not flow
Now evening, four degrees centigrade, dark, westerly winds
And the Baltic rushing whitely to the edge of the town
It will rain tonight, but I will not fly in my dreams
As the winds buffet this house,
And innocence has been murdered
While we rest here, our words unflowing
I cannot fly west, cannot help
Know nothing yet of the death of a colleague's daughter
A 17-year-old who entered Le Bataclan
On a false pass and was shot.
Still I know nothing of the blood and broken flesh
Le Carrion, Le Petit Cambouge,
La Belle Equippe, Stade de France,
Out there in the night the wind moves
Like a rampaging animal among winter's birches
Finds no holding place
Except where it strikes the wall of this house.
I will survive the night as the young are murdered
As the killers shoot themselves
As hatred takes its stroll through Paris.
Tomorrow it's hard to believe
That I can try to write again
Or any of us

Sacred Sea – Visby

A white ship anchors in the harbour.
Seagulls perch with tucked-in wings
on coils of rope; cafes leak their scent
to the darkening hour. Rain expected,
the town is folding down to darkness.

As the storm rolls through the streets,
leaves fall to the gutter's mouth.
I hesitate to peer at these Byzantine discards—
bronze, red-veined—someday,
I too will be pure leaf, leaving only residue.

I consider my restive escapes
to this or that refuge, turn shoreward again,
in search of winter in sinuous drifts,
my head bent to snowy pages,
the quick spark of a colder sun.

October Vision

Here is my father in the kitchen
on the eve of masks and apples,
creamy Brazils and crinkled walnuts,
the nutcracker pressing hard
but not enough to shatter
the moist interior.

My hand plunges
in a filled crate of apples,
raises the reddest from beneath.
Beyond the window,
the wild cat we used to feed
slinks down from the high wood,

the hills crouching close,
while a mist curls thick paws
around the house.
Low sky, no hint of a wind,
today's ochre-lit lanterns of leaves
reveal the sacred veil.
It parts to my keeping, my watch.

The Kitchen Girl's Pumpkin

The mother plant lies shrivelled,
puckered as an umbilical cord after birth,
exhausted by this hefty youngster
that glows brazenly through morning fog.

She studies the single yellow gourd,
flesh that yields to her grimed fingernail
but does not break; hollow sound
when she taps it with a knuckle,
its life–dense weight.

Next year, she promises
to experiment with the plants:
one for the glasshouse, the rest
in open garden, taking their chances
in vagrant soil.

At night, on her narrow settle,
she feels only solid heat.
Her dreaming mind already harvests seeds
scoured loose by a santoku knife,
composes violent soups
for the long table upstairs.

Mary of St Médiers

for Mary Lynch

Her house in the old *Mairie,* a temple
To everything the people did not want;
What was dumped, sold cheaply, discarded.
Here, to pass through the rooms is a burlesque
Revolution, door through door;
You swim towards old mirrors
That distort reflections, past weeping wallpapers
And Chinese screens.
Mountains of clothes her time-piece,
Bought at one market, in wait of the next,
These decades are not really for sale,
The people who wore them long dead
And Mary still in the full of vitality.

In the inmost chamber, her violated dolls
Invite the rush of desire some women feel
In late adulthood, to cradle something small,
Then place it aside for admiration.
Heads are missing. Or arms.
Sometimes a well-dressed torso is enough,
They can imagine the rest.
Worst or best, depending, are the African dolls,
A quintet, once used for healings, fertility,
And one in particular for who-knows-what:
You would not have it in a quiet home,
That murk-brown face in greedy flitters,
The tufted, frozen eyes,
As if knife-attacked in the underworld
When the witch doctor's incantations
        Failed.

Outside, hairy dogs circle and parade
The paths, rescued from open roads, cruelties.
They await her kindnesses—a chaise longue,
A high and giant bed that would
Take the world in if she but waved her hand.
Autumn sun nudges at yellowing trees,
Wasps mizzle on the air, a scorpion sidles
From beneath a rock, beetles crackle along
Paths, at home in the old Mairie.

Dolphins

for Bridget Flannery, artist

We were watching from the shore,
    as he kayaked in the bay,
        heading for the shallows.
His twelve-year-old shoulders
    had lately begun
        to bulk, stretch, and
in his eyes no shadows.
    It happened suddenly—
        a pod, first one dolphin
arced beside the vessel,
    and he smiled, kept paddling.
        Then a noose of them
burst from the calm,
    up and over his head,
        down the other side, beneath,
swept up again to fly
    a circle of salt-spattered light,
        sea-crystal over him
as if at play. He, startled, went still,
    then alarmed, cried out
        to us on shore,
though we smiled and waved
    in excitement. Then
        a sudden flip and
plunge to the depths,
    the whole pod bearing
        the secret message
that was him, to the deeps,
    beyond the hotel
        on the cliff, beyond
domino rows of beach homes,
    away from us, his family.
        He was growing.

There are no mermaids,
    and soft-grazing sea-cows
        will not come either.
But they came, emissaries,
    preparing him for sirens
        on land, the clear eyes
of seeking girls
    who'd try him.
        One way or another.

Elegy for a Writer

Remembering Eileen Battersby

a woman I knew is laid out today
not in a parlour or fine room
but in a stable

her dun horses have galloped
home across acres of stars
where they graze among unicorns
    they bear pearl fragments from the horn
of this gentlest of beasts

in the stable   barn-owls have scooped
that pearl to weave a bridle
for her right hand
tenderly tethering to her fingernails
       the horses' nostrils flare close
in soft breaths to the shape of a head
that would lean into their necks and croon
alone! alone! before riding out

their dark hooves will beat the earth
sense a passage to open pasture
bearing her and her millions of words
across the heavens

a woman I knew is laid out today,
not in a parlour or fine room
but in a stable

Portrait of my Brother-in-law's Spare Room

for Pat Nugent

The picture here, of sampans and fisher folk,
hasn't made it to the living area,
nor has that black Chinese lacquered tallboy
with traceries of willow and water,
retrieved from the tail ends of your marriage,
like salvage. On the floor, the rug once bartered for

in Irkutsk, shows little sign of wear,
another discard. Your many spare shirts
are stacked in white piles within the drawers,
criss-crossed so that the collars do not crumple
under pressure. Outside this room,
you're a local again, all midland drawl,

drink coffee as your blown left eye adjusts
to a pub soccer game. Behind that dark pupil
your neurons reboot the default stories,
Far East years, intersecting episodes
of Kowloon, and the Irish politician
who once visited. You recall too,

a Chinese fascination with your starry,
blue-eyed children, their dangling, unruly
blonde curls. Now, the remnants are de-fragged,
for visitors only, who know of your journey
on the Trans-Siberian Railway,
when you brought home such jewels

as could never be worn, then crashed the car
in a lacerating winter skid. You still shake hands
like a businessman, still speak Mandarin,
but forget the minutes of your days.
They drift like fallen willow leaves
into the canal, not the Yangtse.

Doorways

Once there, a week was delicious, slow to pass,
grandparents and aunts open-armed
to us, who arrived each year on holiday.
The trek south from Monaghan long, exciting,
the Blackstairs mountains a final sign
that we were almost there. Once through the door,

across oil-scented anterooms, kitchen door
wide, and grandmother remarking how I'd pass
for my mother's younger sister, a sign
of times ahead: resisting, I armed
myself against what mother thought exciting,
fiercely, much later taking holidays

in places that aggrieved her—French holidays,
my love for *la France profonde,* welcoming door
to a bohemian way; but for now, father's parents' exciting
habits—candles, chamber pots & calisthenics—I passed
through 1930s rooms, the marble mantle armed
with gentle *art deco* vases, aunt's violin, a sign

that music mattered here in Ballyneale, a sign
of quiet reflection. My other aunt, the nun, her holiday
brought abruptly to an end, wept quiet tears, armed
herself again for convent life, through the grim door
to where she pined silently for laughter, a pass
to something glamorous, exciting.

She later dyed her hair, (Morgan's Pomade), exciting
enough to become blonde beneath the veil, her sign
of entering the *world*. And then our week would pass,
I'd weep in the car at the end of the holiday,
for the fading, soft, Munster voices at the door,
and Margaret and I now filled again, tenderly, armed

to return north, to school and all, armed
again, recalling the house, the hens, exciting
times with doting aunts, who teased us behind the doors.
As in life, the hard and the soft, secret signs
between adults, mother tolerating that week, a holiday
we never wanted to end; and then it passed.

I still think of the armed exemplar of aunts on holiday,
walks on lanes they made exciting, spirited signs
before we went north to pass again through other doors.

The Future Wears a Yellow Hat

The past, an underworld chamber.
We visit habitually,
drunk from the river
of forgetfulness,
brows perplexed as we struggle
with bodies—ailing,
misaligned—
that let us down.

That easy touch,
that musk, a morning sigh
and shared cafetière,
escape our senses.
We erase the future too,
storied with our lives,
ignorant of dead loves
waving hands and hats
to catch our attention.
If we remember the future—
quickly, like skinning a rabbit,
exposing the bone—
we will never look back.
It greets us effortlessly,
waving its yellow hat
as we cross a high bridge
from opposite directions,
smiling—

Acknowledgements

Acknowledgements are due to the editors, anthologists, scholars, producers, and academics who have accepted my poems for inclusion in a wide range of outlets, in print, online, and on radio. Sincere thanks to poet Patrick Chapman for his welcome suggestions, to poets and authors Grace Wells and Nessa O'Mahony, to writer and publisher Richard Kraviec, to writer Kevin Myers and to Dr Richard Hayes.

Poetry Ireland Review (issues 120, 122, 126, 129); *The Irish Times*; *Sunday Miscellany* (RTE Radio 1, producer Sarah Binchy); *Words Lightly Spoken* (podcast, producer Claire Cunningham); *The Poetry Programme* (RTE Radio 1, producer Claire Cunningham); RTE Lyric FM *CultureFile* (producer, Eithne Hand); *Crannóg*; *Cyphers*; *The Irish Examiner*; *The Stony Thursday Book*; *SurVision*; *Live Encounters*; *Banshee* (issue 8, spring/summer 2019); *The Poetry Bus* (issue 8 2019); *RAUM* (Scotland, 2017); *Frogmore Papers* (UK, 2017); *Prole* (UK, 2018); Candlestick Press *Ten Poems about Brothers* (2018, UK); *Revista Itaca Dublin* (2017, ed. Viorel Ploesteanu); *The Curlew* (2018, Wales); *Poetry London*; *The London Magazine*; *Orbis* ("Readers' favourite poem", 2016); *BBC Radio 3*; *The North Special Irish Edition* (2018, editors Nessa O'Mahony and Jane Clarke); *New Hibernia Review* USA; *Prelude* USA; *The Matador Review* USA; *The Café Review* USA; *Studi Irlandesi* (Italy, 2017 editor Fiorenzo Fantaccini, foreword Giovanna Tallone); *Études Francaises* (2019, France, editors Catherine Conan and Flore Coulouma).

Work is also included in the following anthologies:

Even the Daybreak: 35 Years of Salmon Poetry, ed Jessie Lendennie (Salmon, 2016); *The Hippocrates Book of the Heart: Initiative for Poetry & Medicine*, ed. Michael Hulse (University of Warwick, 2016); *Washing Windows? Irish Women Write Poetry*, ed. Alan Hayes (Arlen House, 2016); *Migrant Shores: Irish, Moroccan & Galician Poetry*, ed. Manuela Palacios (Salmon Poetry 2017); *Metamorphic: 21st Century Poets Respond to Ovid*, eds Nessa O'Mahony, Paul Munden (Recent Work Press in association with the International Poetry Studies Institute at the University of Canberra, 2017); *The Lea-Green Down: Irish Poets Respond to Patrick Kavanagh*, ed Eileen Casey (Flaming Arrow Press, 2018); *Writing the Future: The Hodges Figgis 250th Anthology*, ed Alan Hayes (Arlen House, 2018); and, *The Stony Thursday Book*, ed. Nessa O'Mahony (Limerick Arts Office 2018).

MARY O'DONNELL is one of Ireland's best known contemporary authors. Her seven poetry collections include *Spiderwoman's Third Avenue Rhapsody*, *Unlegendary Heroes*, both with Salmon Poetry, and *Those April Fevers* (Ark Publications). Her poetry is available in Hungarian as *Csodak földje* with the publisher Irodalmí Jelen Könyvek. Fiction includes the novels *The Light Makers* (reissued in 2017 with 451 Editions), *The Elysium Testament* and *Where They Lie*. A volume of essays on her work, *Giving Shape to the Moment: The Art of Mary O'Donnell*, was published in 2018 (Peter Lang). Her third short story collection, *Empire*, was published by Arlen House in 2018. An essay, "My Mother in Drumlin Country", published in *New Hibernia Review* during 2017, was listed among the Notable Essays and Literary Nonfiction of 2017 in *Best American Essays* (Mariner). She is a regular invited guest at literary festivals and events both in Ireland and internationally. An elected member of Aosdana, Ireland's affiliation of artists, she lives in County Kildare.

salmonpoetry

Cliffs of Moher, County Clare, Ireland

"Like the sea-run Steelhead salmon that thrashes upstream to its spawning ground, then instead of dying, returns to the sea—Salmon Poetry Press brings precious cargo to both Ireland and America in the poetry it publishes, then carries that select work to its readership against incalculable odds."

TESS GALLAGHER

The Salmon Bookshop
& Literary Centre

Ennistymon, County Clare, Ireland

"Another wonderful Clare outlet."
The Irish Times, 35 Best Independent Bookshops